THE
BEAR

DANIÈLE HEYMANN

from the film by JEAN-JACQUES ANNAUD
photographs by MARIANNE ROSENSTIEHL

Translated by Sarah B. Pettit

SIDGWICK & JACKSON
LONDON

First published in Great Britain in 1989 by
Sidgwick & Jackson Limited
1 Tavistock Chambers, Bloomsbury Way
London WC1A 25G.

First published in France by Editions Grasset & Fasguelle
First published in USA by St Martin's Press

ISBN 0 283 99870 9

Design by Richard Oriolo

Photo credits: page 5, top, Jean-Philippe Varin; page 40, Xavier Castano.

THE BEAR

Youk thanks Jean-Jacques Annaud, Claude Berri, Gérard Brach and Josée Benabent-Loiseau, without whom he would not have had this adventure.

It was the most beautiful morning ever. Youk, the bear cub, felt all grown up — or almost grown up. His mother gave him a nudge. She had a special treat planned for today. "Come on, hungry. We're going to find some honey."

The honey was far away and high up in the rocks, and Youk had trouble climbing. Climbing and running, he had the same problem — in front he'd be fine, but his back end just couldn't keep up.

Youk's mother was waiting for him by a big boulder. He could hear it buzzing and humming. "They're here," said Mum. "Who?" said Youk. "The bees." "But I don't want bees! I want honey!" "Little Youk," said his mother, "you can't have one without the other. No sun without rain, no day without night."

Mum ducked her head under the rocks and dug a bit with her paws. She worked busily. Finally, she reappeared, her nose glistening with golden honey. All around her flew the bees, stripey creatures that buzzed and stung, but Youk hardly noticed them. He sat in front of his mum and licked her face. Honey, oh, honey! It was so delicious. Sweeter than the sunshine!

Youk's mother went back again and again for honey. Youk's tummy was puffed up and stung all over and his tongue was all red and droopy from licking — but he didn't want to stop.

Suddenly, pebbles started to hail down around them. Mum couldn't hear because her head was in among the rocks and she was scraping around with her paws. High above her, Youk saw a boulder beginning to teeter. At first, it looked pretty; it balanced as though it were as light as a feather. But then it was tumbling, and falling — it was huge and deadly. It crashed down and the mountain groaned.

Then everything was quiet. Youk's mother was lying on the ground, as motionless as the stone itself. She was limp and stiff at the same time. Youk was frightened. His mother looked awful, but he loved her. He wanted to run away, but he didn't want to leave her. He called "Mum?" but she didn't answer. All he heard was the echo of his own voice. "Mum…Mum…"

"Come on, Mum," he called, "the sun's gone cold. It's all small and red. Please, don't leave me." It was dark now. To Youk, his mother's fur looked black. He felt black inside. He felt like he'd swallowed a pine cone.

When the sky grew dark, Youk's mother used to say, "Little Youk, the sun has gone to bed, now it's your turn." He would always play a little longer, because who can go to bed when they're told to? Now he wanted to snuggle into Mum's fur. He wanted to sleep the way she had taught him, close up against her, but he couldn't. He didn't hear her evening lullabye, her rocking and soothing song. "Youk, my cuddly little bear, Youk, the one with the fuzzy red hair…." He lay down by himself on the ground. Mum….

      "I'm all alone," Youk thought as he awakened. He did not know whom to tell this to or, for that matter, who had told it to him. Maybe it was the morning breeze that came fresh and new every day. "I'm all alone, and I'm sad," Youk said to himself.

      "You can't be *all* sad," said the morning breeze to Youk. "You can't be all sad when the stream is close by and you've just had a drink from it. And when this stream is so clear that you can look into it and see a little bear, drinking, and above him, floating and flashing, a squadron of hovering dragonflies.

      "You can't be all sad when the buttercups leave traces of their golden pollen dust on you. You can't be all sad when I, the morning breeze, tickle your ears, and when the grass is full of things that squeak and buzz and leap and run and live. And you live, too."

The breeze made Youk feel a little better. Hey, he thought, there's a flying flower. A flower with two identical petals that flutter and flap. This way, over this way, butterfly! I'm following you. Not so high! Please, not so high, and wait for me! And in trying to catch this pretty, winged flower, Youk slipped and tumbled. It hurt a bit, but it was fun. One minute he was facing the sky, the next he was face down in the dirt. He rolled and rolled, until he couldn't figure out if it was his head or the ground that was spinning. When he finally stopped, his fur was covered with twigs and nettles. He felt like a little porcupine or a prickly bush.

Then another creature caught his eye. "Look. What kind of animal is this? I've never seen anything like it before," Youk said. "It's certainly disgusting. There's no hair! And it's tiny and slimy and green." (Youk had never seen a frog before.) He went to trap it, just to play with it, but away it jumped. It took a big, round hop, like a gazelle or the curve of a rainbow, and was gone.

Youk found more games to play. He ran and gambolled. He nibbled at willow shoots, chicory roots, and iris bulbs. Then he discovered a stone that walked. When Youk tried to play with it, its head popped out and said, "Please, a little respect! After all, I am the eldest one around here." It was old, all right, and wrinkled and wizened. "Who are you?" said Youk. "I'm a tortoise," said the stone.

What Youk saw next made him blink his eyes. I must be dreaming. I'll soon wake up, he thought. In front of him, at some distance but not too far, was a gigantic bear. A bear even bigger than Mum. How was that possible? All of a sudden something inside Youk began to pound. It felt like the crazy tapping of a woodpecker's beak.

The bear stood upright and bellowed, shaking its head back and forth in a long, agonized movement. He's hurt, thought Youk, he's hurt.

So, as fast as he could, he began to trot toward the wounded giant. The closer he got, the bigger and more powerful the bear seemed. Now Youk could see that the bear's flank had a bad puncture wound and that his thick red fur was matted with blood. It was a round, deep hole that no animal could have made. Again the bear bellowed in pain.

Youk's heart beat faster and faster. "I'm not all alone anymore," he said, or at least he tried to, but all that came out was a grunt. He flattened out on his belly, and wiggled along like a caterpillar, as a sign of respect for the bear.

Youk was close up now. The bear continued to send out enormous, loud cries that echoed off the mountains. His mouth was a big red cavern crammed with white spears. Youk got even closer. Too close. The bear's paw plucked him off his feet and sent him flying twenty paces as if he were an acorn. He landed with a thump that made his head spin.

Youk looked around. Where had the bear gone? Groaning, grumbling, and gasping for air, the big bear loped off toward the stream. He dropped into the water heavily. With only his head above the current, he let himself be carried downstream. Youk stood at the edge of the rolling water, carefully dipping a toe into the waves. Where had the bear gone? He couldn't see him. In all his agitation, Youk dove in. Help! thought Youk. How do the fish do it? I'm certainly no fish. I've got water up my nose. I'm choking! I'm drowning!

Finally, a rock. Youk grabbed hold, scrambled on, and came to rest on his little island, soggier than a pond lily. Where had the bear gone?

Over there, a bit further away. The big bear was tucked into a mud-hole, but he wasn't moving at all. Maybe he's dead, thought Youk, hoping that wasn't true.

Youk waded over to the big bear and looked at him. His eyes were closed. He had sunk into the cool mud to soothe the fire in his wounded flank. Once in a while, he tried to lift his head, but didn't have the strength. His ears perked up; he sensed Youk nearby. He wanted to scare him off, but didn't have the energy this time.

"I'm not scared," Youk told himself. It surprised him that he wasn't for there, only a beaver's tail away from him, was a huge mass of bear. And so was that open wound. Youk remembered what his mother used to do when he was hurt. He settled his soft lips and his wet black nose against the wound, and he set to licking and licking with all his heart. He licked just the way Mum had done. He could still hear her: "I'm licking and rocking you, Youk. I'm licking and rocking you, Youk. Squishy, squashy tongue will heal the pain, by the morning you'll be right as rain."

The big bear opened his eyes. He saw the drenched cub taking care of him. He saw the little bear who had to face many dangers, including a mighty bad temper, to lay a red tongue on his suffering.

And so, the wounded bear took a deep breath and, when his turn came, he gave Youk a bear kiss: He licked Youk's tiny nose with his huge, rough tongue. It was a kiss full of peace and friendship. Youk felt as if he were melting. He teetered with joy. He felt he was being pushed off balance by a warm wave that covered him and washed away all his fears, his sadness, and his loneliness.

"All right, you little water rat, let me sleep," said the big bear. "I'm not called water rat," replied Youk, "my name is Youk." "Well, I'm Kaar," said Youk's new friend. Then he dozed off.

The next morning was radiant. Kaar's wound was almost healed. Youk horsed around while Kaar took a ceremonious bath. During it he instructed little Youk on a thousand important subjects:

How juicy grubs burrow into the thorny bark of the acacia tree. How blueberries make your tongue turn dark with their sweet juice. How to catch fish in a mountain stream. How vast the earth is, and how the migrating birds bring stories of far-off places. Or how the springtime is more than just the season of flowers and fragrances, but is also the season of love.

And how love carries no warning; it cannot be explained and it cannot be learned. It makes you sweeter than maple syrup, lighter than bird's down, and more powerful than the giant puma.

After all that, off went Kaar without warning. "Wait for me!" cried Youk, but Kaar waited for no one. Youk did what he could to keep up, gasping and tripping over rhododendron roots. Finally, he caught up to the big bear and did an ecstatic little jig, covering him in a flood of hugs and kisses.

"Anyone would think you hadn't seen me in at least two moons," Kaar laughed. Then he said, "Come closer, do you hear anything?" Kaar turned both his ears and nose in the direction of the wind. "Can't you smell anything, little one?" "I don't hear or smell a thing," answered Youk, "What —" An imperial swipe of the paw silenced the tiny cub.

"Be quiet. Do like I do." Kaar sank down, flattened out, and started a slow creep toward the undergrowth ahead. His eyes were bright, his muscles tensed. He moved silently, never losing the scent. Youk copied him carefully.

Kaar stopped. He was at attention, poised to attack. A branch crackled. In one movement, claws thrashing, fangs bared, Kaar launched himself into the thicket. Youk couldn't figure out what was going on, but let slip a growl as if it might help.

From the undergrowth into which Kaar had disappeared, Youk heard fierce sounds and shrill cries. Then nothing at all. He stood and peeked. Out of the grass stuck the antlers of a creature Youk couldn't see. The antlers edged closer; they twisted and shuddered. They belonged to a stag Kaar had just killed. He was dragging it toward the clearing.

Youk felt overwhelmed by a ferocious excitement. His mouth was watering, his body was shivering, and his belly was gripped by a strange hunger. He caught up to Kaar and together they began to eat hungrily. Youk had never been more ravenous. His snout burrowed into the steaming innards. Blood matted his fur. Kaar, too, was tearing into the fresh meat. "Can't beat hunting, can ya, little guy?" he said.

Finally, the two satisfied bears settled back against the carcass for a siesta. Kaar blasted thunderous snores while, at his side, Youk made tiny snuggly sounds. The noises all around them blended into a symphony of rustling leaves, chirping crickets and twittering birds.

Suddenly, Kaar awakened and shook his little friend. "Youk," he said, "the wind is full of scary smells. When I close my eyes, I see a decaying coyote corpse swarming with maggots. But it's not that. I close my eyes again and see a pink salmon rotting at the riverside. Greenhead flies are buzzing all over it. But that's not it either. Youk, if you ever smell this terrible odour and can't identify it, take a good noseful — you'll know that man isn't far away."

"That's pretty disgusting," said Youk. But he didn't know what man was. He went back to sleep.

A while later, he woke up and found his furry pillow gone. The stag had disappeared and so had Kaar! He wasn't really scared yet, but he decided he'd better find his missing friend. He remembered Kaar's lesson and put his nose into the wind, looking for a familiar scent. He couldn't find any smells, only a distant clamour of sounds. "That must be Kaar! Here I come," said Youk, hurrying down the slope and across the hillside to the flower-filled valley below. Just as he was about to burst across the springy meadow, two loud cries froze him in his tracks. Youk thought he recognized Kaar's voice, but it seemed different, a mixture of pleading and bravery. And whom did the other voice belong to? It was higher and more shrill.

Youk looked around, but he couldn't see where the sound came from. Undefeated, he climbed the nearest pine and from its top found a bird's-eye view into the meadow. There was Kaar; but who was that with him?

At the opposite end of the field, amid the primroses, the wild pansies, and the bluebells, was a golden she-bear. The beautiful Iskwao did not even glance at Kaar, but preferred to rest on her big behind and casually snack on ants.

What's wrong with Kaar? He's acting so oddly, thought Youk. His big friend was showing off, yodelling madly and balancing on his hind legs like a tubby ballerina.

Iskwao, of course, was not paying the tiniest bit of attention to him. She contented herself with lazily rolling around on the velvet grass and warming her soft tummy in the sun.

From up on his perch Youk watched the scene below and thought, Grown-ups and their silly games. This is boring.

     Youk was right. Kaar took a step toward Iskwao and she one toward him. They got close up and pretended to squabble. There seemed to be a lot of noise. And a lot of, "I'll give you a slap," or, "I'll bite your neck," or, "I'll try to catch your tail, but don't you dare put your snout there."

     "More and more boring," said Youk.

     Just then, Iskwao escaped from her suitor and returned to digging in the anthill. Kaar, by now crazy with love and frustration, let out a cry. He clutched a tree trunk and shook it in his frenzy.

     Youk was fed up. "All right, that's enough," he said. He got down from his perch and headed off in search of a snack.

"I'll find something tasty to munch on," said Youk. "It could be something crisp or crunchy or sugar-coated. Or all three. It's beautiful out and I'm in no hurry. Time to eat a lot, get fat and not worry...." Over by the rhododendrons, Youk found something that looked tasty. Could it be a mushroom? It looked delicious, with a stalk that was tender and pearly white, and a cap that was red with elegant white spots. "Hold it right there, mushroom, I'm going to snack on you."

The first bite was a disappointment. The mushroom didn't taste nearly as good as it looked. It was spongy and didn't have much taste. Maybe even a little moldy. Youk continued to chomp anyway. I'm not sure why, he thought, I could be eating anything else. Suddenly, he felt a touch feverish and strangely lazy. He was all floppy and limp. It was time to stretch out and relax.

The mushroom had a very curious effect. Youk had wild dreams, hallucinations. Hairy frogs. Purple clouds that laughed and beat their bellies. He saw a waterfall of warm milk falling into a carpet of open mouths! A blue snake walking along speedily with its head tucked under its arm. "Oh my! Oh my!" said Youk. In front of him he saw a transparent wall, a giant spider's web, and he was going right through it.

And suddenly he took off and flew over the undergrowth. The silky ferns shook their stalks at him and shouted, "Long live Youk! Long live Youk!" He felt as light as a ladybird.

It was a dizzy and dozy little bear that Kaar found some time later.

In another part of the mountains, two men were on the trail. They made their way without a word. They had climbed countless narrow mountain passes and spent too many seasons in the forests and valleys. Their skins were the colour of dead leaves and the brims of their hats were as worn from rain and sun as a beaver's belly.

These men were the hunters.

Their pack mule was already weighed down with bearskins. But

they had sworn to come back and get the bear they had missed before. They had hit him with a bullet, but he got away.

      They rested for a while in the clearing. The elder, Bill, had a grey, grizzled beard. He sucked a beat-up pipe through tobacco-stained teeth. The younger, Tom, was as ruddy as a squirrel but not half as mischievous. While they sat, Tom cleaned his rifle, a Winchester. On a stone its polished parts lay flat, glinting menacingly.

The camp was quiet. The pack mule stood nearby, lifeless bear heads hanging on one side, empty paws on the other. The pack of dogs nestled close to the fire. There were the sleek black hounds and then there was Dixie, Tom's curly blonde dog. Finally the men got up.

"Wanna go?"

"Yeah, let's go."

The hunters broke camp. They plodded up the narrow mountain pass. Not a word passed between them; their thoughts were on killing the bear. Bill was in the lead and when he raised his arm, the little caravan came to a stop. Bill grinned without losing his pipe. He had just spotted some droppings on the path and they were bear droppings. He could tell by examining them that the bears had been there not long before them. "An hour," he said. "Maybe an hour and a quarter."

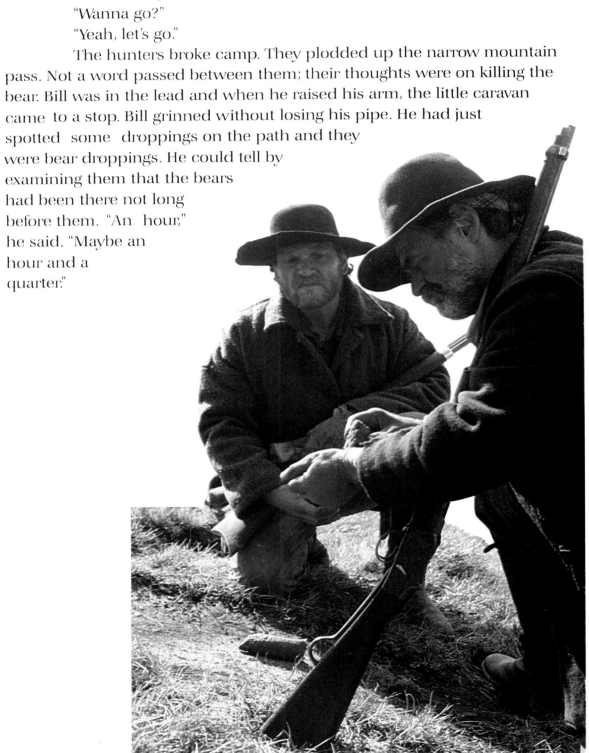

Kaar and Youk knew the hunters were nearby. They could smell men and dogs and mules. And then they heard the dog pack.

The mountain cried out. Loud, hate-filled barking echoed and rolled among the rocks. Kaar climbed higher and higher, faster and faster, toward a sheer, creviced rock face. Youk followed along bravely until he was blocked by an impossibly steep rock. He tried standing on the tips of his toes, grabbing and pulling with all of his might, but nothing helped. He could go no higher.

Kaar reached the top and looked back. He saw two tiny round ears and two frightened brown eyes peering over the rock's edge. "Hold on, buddy," he said. "I'll be back for you." He would lead the dogs away from Youk.

Finally, Kaar reached his goal, a natural clearing strewn with boulders. Here he waited, ready for the enemy.

Youk had slid into a crevice and couldn't see much. He was trembling. And then the battle began. Youk could hear a terrible racket: screams and snarls, accompanied by panting. The clearing was a blur of paws, fur, fangs, dust, drool, and blood.

Silence returned. Youk didn't know what was going on. What had happened to the pack of dogs? He decided to take a peek. Look, other animals are coming, he thought. They're walking on their hind legs like we do. But what ugly feet, all smooth and leathery. And skinny! Uh! What a stink! Uh! It smells like rotten meat! Uh! They're men!

Youk sneaked out of his hiding place. He wanted to find Kaar and stop this fiery nightmare full of blood and scary moments. He wanted to go back to the simplicity of the forest and its peaceful games, its wild raspberries, cool baths and chicory roots, funny pranks, juicy black ants. He wanted to play with Kaar and listen to the goldcrests singing in the morning.

With his nose to the ground and his rear in the air, Youk hurried along his friend's trail. Then an awful noise stopped him dead in his tracks. Swallowing up the hillside were the two shadows. He recognized the smooth leather feet and yowled, "Kaar!" Suddenly, everything went black.

Black, it was all black, and what a smell. The hunters had thrown a jacket over Youk to capture him. "My, my," said Tom, "look how this little worm wiggles." "Just you wait, you dirty coyotes," spat Youk. And he clawed and bit, he wheezed, he panted, and he struggled. Kaar would be proud of me, he thought, which made the clawing, biting, and struggling begin anew. "Nasty little worm. I'll get you," said Bill, hitting him again and again on his snout, his head, and his bottom.

"You're not hurting me, you rotten coyote. No, you're not hurting me," whimpered Youk. But under the dark folds of the black cloth, he was blinded and defenseless. Hurt and frightened, he rolled himself up into a tiny shivering ball. He was sure Kaar was looking for him but he was trapped and uprooted. He was a prisoner.

He heard crackling, snapping, whinnying, yapping. "There are monsters everywhere in this enemy night," said Youk. There were the horses with their sagging bellies, legs like posts, teeth as yellow as beavers' and big, drippy eyes. And then, the dogs, who were always angry. They had pointy fangs, cuts all over, and garbage breath. Monsters....

The men were bedded down for the night. Youk felt tired too, but how could he give up on Kaar? How could he fall asleep when ghosts danced through the firelight shadows in the clearing? Would he ever see his friend again?

The wind knew the answer. The wind was the forest's breath. It rustled through the trees in a secret night-time dance. And tonight, the wind carried another breath. It was Kaar's. The great bear stood quietly, watching the campsite, hidden among the low branches. He whispered to Youk, who could not hear, "Little one, we will meet again. Little one, we'll go to Plutar's wild mountain streams, where you can fish for the moon and the leaping salmon. We'll play in the marsh orchids, and hunt the timid elk and the racy hare. Little friend, I'll come and find you."

The sky grew light. Wisps of fog trailed from the low branches and the lark sang a hoarse song. The camp awakened. Tom opened a can of condensed milk, poured it into a pan, and set it down near the sleeping bear cub.

Youk's nostrils twitched. He woke up, almost overpowered by the sweet smell. His mouth watered and he couldn't help licking his chops. "Hey, you're smiling!" said Tom. He pushed the pan closer to Youk, who poked out his nose and then his tongue. Next, he reared back on his legs and moved his paws through the air like a show dog. Tom laughed, "Come on, little clown, try a sip."

Youk licked the man's hand before he would taste the milk. Ooh! he thought. By the belly of the giant cougar, as Kaar would say, nothing can beat that. It's thicker, creamier, and more sugary even than honey.

And he lapped and lapped as if his life depended on it. He could think of nothing else but this smooth, sweet warmth. It was like an

 addiction. The pan was empty, but still Youk licked. He banged the black metal like a tambourine, asking for more. For Youk, the sweet drink was like a drug, one that would turn him into the slave of men. He didn't notice or maybe he chose not to. These men killed his brothers with one hand and fed him with the other. But Youk told himself, "No honey without bees, no day without night."

The men had left to track Kaar again. There was no need to tie Youk up. They knew the cub was theirs now, attached to them by an invisible rope. At the campsite, everything was still. Youk felt ornery. He looked around. On the ground, as carefully woven and laced as any bird's work, was a big nest.

Youk sneaked. He snooped. In the nest were two pairs of pants, an old yellowed photograph of a girl, a dirty hanky, a pouch of tobacco, three socks, a magnifying glass, a knife with a bad blade, a clean hanky, a compass, and a ragged book called *Hunting the Grizzly*, which didn't taste very good. So all in all, nothing really interesting.

What else was there? Ah! Another big nest. Sneaking. Snooping. A little dried fish, not enough even to line your stomach, and some strips of caribou as tough as holly root. White powder that made you thirsty and black powder that made you sneeze. How disappointing. But there was one more thing to try....

Bull's eye! Youk had discovered the store of milk. The white nectar spurted and dribbled. Youk dived into the sticky, sweet mess and rubbed it everywhere — on his nose, his ears, his paws. He was drunk. He reeled and collapsed on a sleeping bag, which burst under him. The milk! The feathers! It was all white and soft! What a wonderful mess! Youk danced in a white cloud.

The hunters had split up. Tom stood on a ridge, his rifle in his hand. "Bear, I'm gonna get you this time," he said. He was looking down on a rugged landscape, scanning the trees for signs of Kaar. Below was a snaking passage of river. The sun blazed down. In the sky, a majestic eagle banked and circled. But there was no bear in sight. Tom was thirsty. Not far down, a spring bubbled. The hunter climbed down to get a drink. He took off his hat and knelt by the stream, cupping the water in his hands and splashing its breathtaking coolness into his face.

Suddenly, an enormous shadow loomed over him. He raised his head and went as white as a sheet. Dead ahead of him was Kaar, a tower of fury and vengeance. Tom could see the clear, still-fresh wounds on his hide Terrible wounds.

"You worm," said Kaar, "You were looking for me? Well, here I am. You're scared, you even smell like it. If I blew on you, you'd fall over. One swipe from me and you'd be cut to ribbons. Have you seen my teeth? If I took a bite, you'd come apart in pieces."

Kaar let out a roar like an erupting volcano. Tom had never felt such terror. He wrung his hands, sobbed, and begged, "Don't kill me."

Coward, thought Kaar, you're no hunter. You're a chicken, a slug. You're not worthy of being my enemy. You make me spit. And Kaar let fly a big glob of spittle that caught Tom right in the face. Then, with a growl, he turned and slowly, calmly, walked away.

Tom was stunned: he was still alive. He felt sick and shaky, but somehow he was not dead. Leaning against a rock, he was violently sick, and then, laughing like a wild hyena with relief, he ran toward where his partner was waiting. Bill saw the wild look in Tom's eyes. "Did you see him?" he asked. Tom could not speak, but pointed in the direction Kaar had gone. The two men hurried off after the bear. Soon they had Kaar within shooting distance, his red fur shining.

Bill let out a victory howl, "Finally, finally!" He raised his rifle and sighted it. But suddenly, Tom stopped him. For a reason he couldn't explain, Tom couldn't let his companion shoot the bear. They watched as Kaar lumbered off, unafraid.

Now, man and beast were even. The beast that had held the man at his mercy spared him. And man had done the same. These were two moments of deep mystery when the age-old battle halted. Two unexpected moments of mutual respect. Two moments when life was victorious over death.

Upon returning to the camp, Tom and Bill discovered a snow-white Youk; a little clown doing an off-balance, happy ballet. He created havoc in their camp, but the hunters didn't have the heart to punish the baby bear.

"Let's go. There's nothing more for us here," said Bill. The horses were saddled, the bags and the pelts were collected. All that remained in the clearing was the black scar of earth from the campfire and an old can of tea.

Tom went over to Youk and scratched his fuzzy head. It felt good. Youk made a friendly noise. "Can't do much with you, little varmint," said Tom. He took the leather collar from around Youk's neck. Youk celebrated his freedom with a hearty tinkle on the collar.

"Saddle up," said Bill. The men moved off into the bluish fog. Youk didn't want to be left behind. "I'll follow them," he thought, and began to bumble along the trail.

"Hey, Tom!" said Bill. "Looks like someone has developed a taste for civilization!" There, on the edge of the forest, sat Youk, a perplexed little ball of breathless fur. His head was cocked in an unhappy way. From far away, Tom waved his arm as if to say, "Go on, get lost. We don't want you." Youk let out a little whine that said, "I should come, right? You want me along, don't you?"

"All right, we're not spending all year here," said Bill. The two men disappeared at a fast gallop into a cleft in the terrain. Youk did not see Tom's last-minute wave of the hand.

Once again, Youk found himself alone with the beautiful scenery. He felt a bit sad, but he also felt more grown up. I'll go where the wind takes me, he thought. He was in no hurry, although he jogged a bit anyway. In his head, there were men and horses, and then they were gone. There was a big bear and then he disappeared.

But there was another animal Youk did not see. High on a steep peak, silent and unmoving with a smooth coat, long legs, honey-toned eyes, spring-action back, and rounded ears, was a puma. And the puma saw Youk.

Like an arrow launched from a bow, the beast leapt and jumped from rock to rock without ever missing his mark. An elegant assassin at work.

The chase was on. Youk fled like a lunatic. He ran faster than he had ever run. He was nothing but a ball of running terror. He made for some rocks, but climbing almost finished him off. The rocks either broke apart under his claws and rained away, or they were all mossy and as slippery as snakeskin. The puma was unstoppable; he leapt with such grace he seemed to be in slow motion. Soon the puma had him cornered by a riverbank.

Even if you're as blind as a bat, fear will do a lot to restore your vision. In a glance, Youk spotted a narrow escape route: overhanging the rushing river was a tree. He sped toward it. By now, he had run so much it felt as if the leather had worn off his feet, and as if fiery cinders had filled his throat.

In a few seconds, the puma had scaled the tree, meowing back at every one of Youk's pathetic cries. The cub backed up, but soon found himself on a long branch that arched out over the river.

The puma would not budge. He too had settled onto the branch, his tail flicking through the air like a whip. He advanced. Youk backed up. Then, with a sickening crack, the branch gave way under his weight.

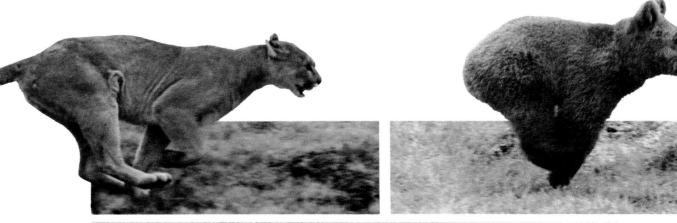

Youk crashed into the water and sank like a stone. He hit bottom and then bobbed back to the surface, spitting, breathing, paddling, and floating. Finally, he grasped onto the fallen branch and let the current whisk him, along with other driftwood, towards dry land. Still the puma leaped after him.

Finally, in Youk's head, a battle cry rang out. The cry that had echoed through the forest since the beginning of time.

"I'm not a baby anymore. I'm a bear and I'm going to fight." He pulled himself up to his full height. He growled, flashing his baby teeth as nastily as he could. He raised his paws like a boxer; he felt brave.

At that instant, the puma sprang forward at lightning speed and swatted the cub's tender nose. Youk's first battle wound.

It hurt! Youk gave out a yell. The puma was caught off guard momentarily by its force. Recovering, he prepared to finish off the noisy cub, until suddenly, just behind Youk, a gigantic silhouette loomed.

Without a moment's hesitation, the angry cat turned tail and sped off. Youk, his nose now bloodied, was thrilled. He had scared a puma away! Now he was grown up!

It was then that he turned around and saw Kaar. The giant was resting on his paws, his heavy head lazily swinging, satisfied and scowling at the vanishing puma. The cub started to launch himself at his protector, only to feel intimidated. Kaar was so big and he, Youk, still so tiny. "Kaar, I'm hurt," he said.

Kaar leaned toward him, sniffed and hugged him. Blood trickled from Youk's nose, but Kaar licked at it until it felt better. The big bear was so forceful in his affection that he almost toppled Youk over. "Hi, little guy," said Kaar.

The Autumn beauty was dizzying. Clouds collected in an indigo sky, while maple and aspen trees released last-minute leaves, golden and fluttering, into the brisk air. Marmots whistled at one another as robins trilled feverishly, preparing for their Winter flight. Busy squirrels shifted stores of acorns, nuts, and pine cones to safe, high places.

"Kaar, do you remember promising that you would take me moon fishing one day?" asked Youk, as they sat by the water.

"You don't forget a thing, do you? Well, let's go now. Look into the water." In the water Youk saw the moon. "How do I catch it?" asked Youk. "No one can tell you that," said Kaar, "it's something you have to figure out on your own."

Youk remembered having caught a heap of rainbow trout one day and imagined it could not be much more difficult. He waited. The moon, all yellow and round, lay before him in the water. He reached out a paw and, there, he had caught it! No, he hadn't caught it. It had split into a thousand shimmering pieces, it was dissolving into arcs in the water. But then, as if to tease him, it returned — a big yellow saucer.

"Kaar! Kaar!" cried Youk in frustration. "The moon is so unkind. I can't catch it."

"Youk, little fella, the moon is not unkind. It's free in the sky. It turns around the earth and soaks up light from the sun. If you lift your head, you'll be able to see it, growing from a sliver to a circle and shrinking again. You can catch trout, because there are millions of those. You can't catch the moon, because it's special and keeps watch up there, next to the stars." Youk promised he wouldn't forget.

The weather was getting cold. Youk's fur had grown thick. "Youk, listen up," said Kaar. "Winter will soon be here. It's the dream season. We have to get ready for it."

He brought Youk to their lair, a well-hidden spot, and went in first. Youk stayed outside a little longer to scratch himself, to play. Kaar turned around in their house, digging little by little to make a nice bed of leaves.

Then he called the cub, who came trotting in and pressed himself against Kaar. Youk's eyes began to close. He could feel tears rising, not sad ones, but the kind that come when you're sleepy. Outside, it was raining, a kind of rain Youk hadn't seen. It fell silently, in quiet flowers, in white petals. I am happy here, Youk thought, in Kaar's warm fur, the way I used to be with Mum. Mum smelled good, like sap, like milk and the forest. Kaar smells stronger, like the blood of wounds and the dust of his battles, but he takes good care of me, and I feel safe. I hope we'll stay here a long time. The whole long Winter.

"There's the snow," murmured Kaar. "It's time to sleep."
And that was the last thing Youk heard.

Winter only seems long to animals that stay awake. To bears carried off in a deep sleep, it is a sure friend. An unknown friend whom you never meet. Winter puts the frost on foxes' pelts and turns them snowy white, but for the bear, it is only the eve of Spring.